World of Islam

Islamic Festivals
and Celebrations

MASON CREST PUBLISHERS
PHILADELPHIA

World of Islam

World of Islam

Islamic Festivals and Celebrations

DOROTHY KAVANAUGH

Editorial Consultants: Foreign Policy Research Institute, Philadelphia, PA

Mason Crest Publishers
370 Reed Road
Broomall, PA 19008
www.masoncrest.com

First printing

1 3 5 7 9 8 6 4 2

Library of Congress Cataloging-in-Publication Data

  Kavanaugh, Dorothy, 1969-
   Islamic festivals and celebrations / Dorothy Kavanaugh.
     p. cm. — (World of Islam)
   Includes index.
   ISBN 978-1-4222-0534-1 (hardcover)
   ISBN 978-1-4222-0800-7 (pbk.)
   1. Fasts and feasts—Islam. I. Title.
   BP186.K365 2006
   297.3'6—dc22

                  2009022081

Dorothy Kavanaugh is a freelance writer whose books include *Islam, Christianity, and Judaism* (2004) and *Islam in Africa* (2006). She lives near Philadelphia.

Table of Contents

Learning About Islam

Today, Islam is the fastest-growing religion in the world. Most estimates now put the worldwide Muslim population at more than 1.4 billion people, which means that approximately one out of every five humans is a Muslim. Islam has surpassed the older religions Hinduism and Buddhism to become the second-largest religion in the world. Only Christianity, with about 33 percent of the global population, has more followers.

The word *Islam* comes from the Arabic verb *aslama*, which means "to submit." The word *Muslim* is also Arabic and refers to a person who submits to the will of Allah, or God. Devout Muslims everywhere submit themselves to Allah daily, both through their faith and by following Islamic law and the commandments in their holy text, the Qur'an. Muslims believe that Allah revealed this scripture to the Prophet Muhammad in the

A mosque, or Muslim place of worship, in Cairo, Egypt. Many mosques have elaborate domes, minarets, and prayer halls. Minarets are tall spires from which a *muezzin*, or prayer leader, notifies Muslims that it is time to pray with a call known as the *adhan*.

Muslims are instructed to study the Qur'an, as this holy book contains the messages Allah is said to have revealed to Muhammad between 610 and 632 C.E. Originally, Muhammad and his followers memorized many of the messages; others were written on scraps of leather or pieces of bone. An authoritative written text was not compiled until the rule of the third caliph, Uthman ibn Affan, about 20 years after Muhammad's death.

seventh century C.E., and that they will be rewarded if they follow Allah's commands.

Over the centuries Muslims collected stories about Muhammad and his earliest followers. These stories, called Hadith, were used to flesh out Allah's commandments, which were recorded in the Qur'an. Islamic teachers and scholars used the Qur'an and Hadith to develop rules regarding the way that Muslims are expected to live. These rules are known as *as-Sunna*, from an Arabic word that means "the path."

There are two major groups of Muslims. The largest sect are known as Sunni Muslims, and they make up about 85 percent of the worldwide Muslim population. Sunni Muslims believe they are obeying the path laid out by Muhammad through his teachings and his exemplary life. Another sect, known as Shiites, make up about 14 percent of the global Muslim population. Shiites broke away from the main group around the year 680 C.E. because of a dispute over leadership of the Islamic community (or *ummah*). Although Shiites and Sunnis agree on the major points of Islamic doctrine, the Shiites developed additional traditions and beliefs that differed from those of the Sunnis.

All Muslims observe five essential religious practices, which are commonly known as the *Arkan al-Islam* (Five Pillars of Islam). The five pillars are the most visible signs of Muslim faith. The most basic of these is a profession of faith (*shahada*), which goes as follows: "There is no god but Allah and Muhammad is the messenger of Allah." This profession affirms the centerpiece of Islam—the religion's monotheistic theology. The other Pillars include prayer (*salat*), charitable giving (*zakat*), fasting during the holy month of Ramadan (*sawm*), and a pilgrimage (*Hajj*) to Islam's holiest place, Mecca, that every Muslim is expected to make at least once during his or her lifetime.

The Daily Prayer Ritual

Muslims offer prayer at different times during each day. The Qur'an mentions three different daily ritual prayers. However, following a tradition established by Muhammad and his early followers, Muslims are expected to perform five daily prayers. When the time for prayer comes, a *muezzin* (prayer leader), issues the *adhan* (call to prayer) from atop a mosque's minaret. When believers hear the call to prayer, they prepare themselves, then bow in the direction of Mecca to pray. The prayers do not have to be recited immediately: Muslims have a certain amount of time in which to perform each specific prayer after they hear the call.

In many Muslim countries, calls to prayer are issued at daybreak, just after noon, at mid-afternoon, at sunset, and in the

Young Indonesian Muslims perform one of the five daily prayers in their mosque.

evening. When Muslims hear the call to prayer, they use small amounts of water to ritually cleanse themselves (and, symbolically, their spirits). They then declare *Allahu Akbar* ("God is Great"), kneel and touch their foreheads on the ground in the direction of Mecca, and recite ritual prayers in Arabic, the language of the Qur'an. This declaration is also known as the *takbeer* in Arabic, and appears on the flags of both Iraq and Iran. Muslims also stand, kneel, stand, and prostrate themselves two to four times, depending on the prayer. To conclude their prayers, Muslims recite the profession of faith and repeat the traditional peace greeting twice, saying "Peace be upon all of you and the mercy and blessings of Allah." Each of the five daily prayers lasts between five and ten minutes. The five daily prayers are as follows (prescribed prayer times in parentheses): *Fajr* (between dawn and sunrise), *Zuhr* (around noon, when the sun is at its highest point in the sky), *'Asr* (during the afternoon), *Maghrib* (after sunset until dusk), and *'Isha'a* (from dusk until dawn).

Prayers outside the five daily ritual prayers in Islam are known as the *nafila*, *sunna*, or *mandub* prayers. These prayers are performed exactly like the proscribed prayers, but they are not mandated. Supplications, known as *du'a*, include spontaneous praise, pleas, and confession. These types of prayers are often heard at Muslim shrines. Believers perform *du'a* by sitting on the floor or ground, holding their hands open, and speaking freely to Allah. Though *du'a* are considered informal and personal, many have been collected and recorded in books.

The Communal Friday Prayer

Muslim tradition calls for believers to pray together when possible. At the very least, Muslim men are expected to recite the noon prayer on Friday at a mosque. Friday is known as *Yawm*

The flags of some predominantly Muslim countries reflect the Islamic heritage of their citizens. For example, the flags of Pakistan (top left) and Turkey (top right) include the crescent moon and star, which are traditional symbols of Islam. The color green is commonly seen in flags of Muslim countries, because green is considered a sacred color in Islam. The flag of Saudi Arabia (middle left) includes the Arabic text of the *shahada*, or Muslim profession of faith. The *shahada* was also incorporated into the top of the coat of arms on the flag of Afghanistan in 2004 (middle right). The borders between the white band and the green and red bands on the flag of Iran (bottom left) are a stylized version of the Kufic script in which the Qur'an is written; the saying *Allahu Akbar* ("God is great") is repeated 11 times on each border. That saying also appears on the flag of Iraq that was adopted in 2008 (bottom right).

al-Jumu'a (literally, "the day of congregation"). Muslims at Friday prayers line up side by side. First, the believers listen as an imam, or prayer leader, preaches a short message based on a verse from the Qur'an. At Jumu'a prayers, the imam often delivers a *khutba* (sermon) on a topic of religious or political relevance. Then the imam directs the Muslims in prayer while facing a niche (*mihrab*) that points in the direction of Mecca. This direction is known as the *qibla* in Arabic. This service usually begins at noon and lasts less than an hour. Afterward, people visit with each other at the mosque.

Muslim men are required to attend the communal Friday prayer, but there is a disagreement in Islamic law on whether women are obligated to attend. Some Islamic extremists, such as the Wahhabis of Saudi Arabia, maintain that women should not attend Friday prayers. More moderate Muslim groups accept the attendance of women at Friday prayers. If women do attend the prayer service, they are often separated from men. This could be a physical separation, such as behind a curtain or in a side room, or a symbolic one, in which the women form prayer lines behind the prayer lines of men.

After attending the Friday service, Muslims may return to their work or they may rest or visit with family and friends for the remainder of the day. In predominantly Muslim countries of the Middle East and Asia, the work week often runs Sunday through Thursday, with Friday and Saturday being days off. In countries like the United States, where the typical work week runs Monday through Friday, devout Muslims may have to request time off to attend the Friday service at the local mosque. Occasionally, in workplaces where a large number of Muslims are employed, a room in the workplace may be prepared for Friday prayers so the workers can conduct the service themselves. When Muslims pray outside a mosque, they use a *sajjada* (prayer rug) to maintain cleanliness while praying. This word comes from the Arabic verb *sajada*, meaning to prostrate oneself.

Guidelines for Daily Living

In addition to the rules for daily prayer, the Islamic scriptures tell Muslims to follow certain guidelines in their daily lives. These guidelines pertain to personal cleanliness and diet.

Ritual ablutions are required of Muslims to create purity of heart before each of the daily prayers. Following a specific commandment in Qur'an 5:6, the believer pronounces Allah's name before washing his or her hands, forearms, face, head, mouth, nose, ears, and feet. The Qur'an also makes clear that Muslims should strive for cleanliness in all other aspects of life as well: "For Allah loves those who turn to Him constantly and He loves those who keep themselves pure and clean" (Qur'an 2:222).

The Qur'an offers few specific instructions for personal hygiene. For example, Qur'an 74: 4 says that believers should keep their clothes clean. However, Muslims also look to the example of Muhammad and his close companions for guidance in their daily lives. This example is called as-Sunna, or "the path." According to the Sunna, Muslims are expected to perform many kinds of personal cleansing. Among these are regular baths, baths before festivals, ritual baths after sex and menstruation, and baths after burying the dead. There are also guidelines for the growth or removal of body hair, regular brushing of the teeth, and for keeping streets and public areas clean and tidy.

Islamic tradition stresses bodily health as essential to purity of heart and a sound intellect. To this end, Muslims are instructed to eat in moderation. Islamic law also prohibits certain foods. Muslims are not permitted to eat pork or other foods that the

Muslims attend a communal prayer service in Kashgar, China.

Qur'an designates as *haram* (forbidden), nor are they supposed to drink alcohol.

Foods that Muslims are permitted to eat must be prepared according to an Islamic ritual that asks for Allah's blessing. Therefore, many Muslims will refuse meat when they are not sure how it was slaughtered. Other Muslims, particularly in the West, do eat commercially prepared meat (other than pork) and say a blessing over it before eating. Meat that meets the Islamic legal requirements is referred to as *halal* (permissible). Halal and haram, however, are terms that do not apply exclusively to dietary habits, but also to daily actions and social behaviors.

The Islamic Lunar Calendar

Muslims observe certain celebrations every year with holidays and feasts. They track their holidays by the Islamic calendar,

The dates of Islamic religious holidays are determined according to a calendar that follows the phases of the moon. This means that each year, Islamic holidays can fall in different seasons. For example, in 2009 the first day of the sacred month of Ramadan was August 21. The date will shift by 10 or 11 days each subsequent year, so that by 2017, Ramadan will begin on May 27.

which follows the phases of the moon rather than the circuit of the sun around the earth. Like the Gregorian calendar used in the West, a year in the Islamic calendar includes twelve months; however, because the cycles of the moon and the sun do not quite match, the Islamic year is about eleven days shorter than the 365-day Western year. Today, people in nearly all Muslim countries follow the western calendar for business but use the Islamic calendar to determine the dates of religious holidays.

Traditionally, a new month in the Islamic calendar begins with the first sighting of a new crescent moon. Just as the Cross and Star of David are the symbols of Christianity and Judaism, respectively, the crescent is the symbol of Islam. Today, it appears on the flags of Algeria, Azerbaijan, Comoros, Malaysia, the Maldives, Mauritania, Tunisia, Turkey, Turkmenistan, Pakistan, and Uzbekistan.The twelve months of the Islamic calendar are Muharram, Safar, Rabi'a al-Awwal, Rabi'a ath-Thani, Jumada al-Awwal, Jumada al-Akhirah, Rajab, Sha'ban, Ramadan, Shawwal, Dhu al-Qa'da, and Dhu al-Hijja.

The Islamic calendar began with the *hijra*, the migration of Muhammad and his followers from Mecca to Medina. According to the Western calendar, the *hijra* occurred on July 16, 622 C.E.; in the Islamic calendar, this migration is said to have occurred on the first day of Muharram in the year 1 A.H. (A.H. is an abbreviation for the Latin phrase Anno Hegirae, meaning "year of the *hijra*"). Muslims consider the *hijra* a fundamental turning point in world history, and believe that the world was in a state of *jahiliyya* (ignorance) prior to the revelation of the Qur'an and Islam.

From Ramadan to 'Eid al-Fitr

The fourth pillar of Islam is the requirement of Muslims to avoid eating and drinking during the daylight hours of Ramadan, the ninth month of the Islamic lunar calendar. Ramadan is considered holy because it was during this month that Muhammad received his first revelation from Allah in 610 C.E. Ramadan is a time for meditation, prayer, and family gatherings. The commandment for Muslims to fast during Ramadan is recorded in Qur'an 2:183: "O you who believe! Fasting is prescribed to you, as it was prescribed to those before you, that you may [learn] self-restraint."

Fasting during Ramadan is required of all capable Muslims past puberty. The elderly, the sick, pregnant women, nursing mothers, and travelers do not have to fast during Ramadan, although they are expected to find another time to complete their fast. Those who are terminally ill, or those who cannot

Muslims participate in Ramadan prayers at the Ethem Bey mosque in Tirane, Albania. Fasting during Ramadan is meant to challenge Muslims to consider their own lives and think about whether they are fully submitting to Allah's will on a daily basis.

Colorful lanterns hang outside a shop in Cairo, Egypt. During Ramadan, Muslims traditionally hang lights and decorate the streets of their towns.

make up the missed days of fasting by fasting on other days, are required to pay a certain amount to charity, which excuses them from fasting.

Because the Islamic calendar is purely lunar, the month of Ramadan can fall at any time of the year. Fasting during the winter is often less difficult because the days are shorter and the weather not as hot, while fasting during the long, hot days of summer can be very difficult, especially for those who work outdoors.

Daily Practices

Each morning during Ramadan, Muslims are expected to eat a pre-dawn meal called Suhur. This recommended meal provides nourishment for the period between dawn and sunset.

Fasting is designed to help increase Muslims' spiritual focus and symbolizes their purification. During the daylight hours, Muslims who are fasting must avoid food, drink, and certain physical activities. Muslims are expected to spend time in prayer during Ramadan, thanking Allah for his blessings and asking forgiveness for sins. Some Muslims make a point of reciting the entire Qur'an during Ramadan, reading one-thirtieth of the holy book each day of the month.

Many Muslims attend their local mosque for the regular evening prayer, which is followed by a special prayer called tarawih, which is recited only during Ramadan. After night falls, Muslims break their fast with a light meal known as the *Iftar*. Some share a late evening meal with members of their extended families. Believers then sleep, waking before dawn to take another light meal, and the process begins again. The Ramadan observance lasts for the entire month.

Voluntary charity (*sadaqa*) for the poor and needy is very important during Ramadan. This often consists of gifts of money or goods to individuals or charitable organizations and ensures that all have enough to eat during the festival at the end of Ramadan.

In most Muslim countries, Ramadan is a very festive time for believers. Cities festoon the streets with lights and flowers, and local businesses decorate their shops. Muslims greet each other with the saying *Ramadan Mubarak!*, which means "a blessed Ramadan." In general, Muslims do not give up their daytime routines, including work, though fasting is considered in part an act of self-discipline by which believers can retreat from everyday life to draw closer to Allah.

While customs associated with Ramadan do vary from country to country, numerous similarities also exist. In many places, candy is distributed to children after the *tarawih* prayer. Certain foods are considered special treats during Ramadan—dates, for example, are widely eaten to break the daily fast, since Muslims believe that Muhammad was fond of dates and often ended his own fasts by eating them. Special foods are also prepared for Ramadan. Qamar ad-din, an apricot paste used for sweets, beverages and pastries in various parts of the Arab world, is also a popular item during Ramadan. In India, for example, a special soup thought to quench thirst and produce energy is served in mosques for the daily breaking of the fast. In some countries, special religious programs or series, known as Ramadaniyyat, air on television during the holy month. Also, most Muslims wear new clothes during Ramadan as a way to symbolize their purification during the season.

The Night of Power

The 27th of Ramadan commemorates the sacred night Laylat al-Qadr ("the Night of Power"). On this night, Muslims remember the first revelation Muhammad received from Allah. According to Surat al-Qadr 97:3–4, on the Night of Power the angels descend to earth at Allah's bidding: "The Night of Power is better than a thousand Months. Therein come down the angels and the spirit by the permission of their Lord, on every errand." Muslims consider this a good time to ask for Allah's blessings. Devout Muslims often pray throughout the entire evening, or stay awake studying the Qur'an.

Muhammad did not specify the exact night to be celebrated as the Night of Power, though 27 Ramadan has become the traditional date. Muhammad did suggest that Laylat al-Qadr should fall in the last 10 days of the month, so some Muslims take this entire period off from work and seclude themselves for intense prayer and study of the scriptures.

During Ramadan, pastries, dates, and other sweets are often eaten at the end of each day's fast.

Muslim residents of the East African country of Eritrea participate in morning prayers during 'Eid al-Fitr, the festival that marks the end of Ramadan.

'Eid al-Fitr

The end of Ramadan is marked by the festival of fast-breaking, known as 'Eid al-Fitr. This festival begins on the first day of Shawwal, the tenth month of the Islamic calendar. On 29 Ramadan, Muslims watch the western horizon for the crescent moon just after sunset; if they do not see the moon, they fast for another day before beginning the festival. In many Muslim countries, 'Eid al-Fitr is a national holiday, and business and government offices usually close for part or all of the celebration. Though 'Eid al-Fitr is considered the lesser of the two major Muslim celebrations (the other is 'Eid al-Adha, which occurs at the end of the Hajj), it is more widely publicized and better known in the West.

A Muslim family in Merv, Turkmenistan, enjoys the 'Eid al-Fitr meal.

The 'Eid al-Fitr festival lasts for three days, during which family members come together to socialize, exchange gifts, and dine on special foods, many of them prepared only for this annual event. Many people wear new clothes and decorate their homes. On the first morning of the festival, Muslims gather in the local mosque to recite a special prayer, called *Salat al-Id*, and hear a sermon. Other services may be held at the mosque and processions of believers wind through the streets. The highlight of the day is a celebratory meal known as *Id Kah*—the first meal Muslims eat during the day after Ramadan. Family and friends gather for this feast, and children are often given gifts and sweets. All Muslims who can afford to give to the poor and needy are expected to do so, just as they are expected to be generous during Ramadan.

3

From Hajj to 'Eid al-Adha

The fifth pillar of Islam is the requirement that at least once in every adult Muslim's lifetime, he or she is expected to make a ritual pilgrimage to Mecca if he or she is physically and financially able. The Hajj, which literally means "to set out for a place," occurs during Dhu al-Hijja, the twelfth month of the Islamic calendar. In any given pilgrimage season, more than 1.5 million Muslims from around the world arrive in Saudi Arabia to make the journey to Mecca. Because the number of pilgrims has grown so large, the Saudi government now regulates the number of pilgrims it will admit from each country. Those who want to make the pilgrimage must apply for entrance to Saudi Arabia. For most of those permitted to make the journey, the Hajj marks a high point of their lives.

The pilgrims' ultimate destination is the shrine known as the Ka'aba, an ancient place of worship that is believed by Muslims

The Ka'aba, an ancient square building in Mecca, is considered by Muslims to be the holiest shrine in Islam. Circling the Ka'aba is an important part of the Hajj ritual.

to have been the site of Allah's covenant with Abraham's son Ishmael. After the Muslims captured Mecca in 630 C.E., Muhammad cleansed the Ka'aba of tribal idols, reclaiming it for Allah and restoring it to its rightful place, according to Qur'an 22: 26–27:

> Behold! We gave the site to Abraham, of the (Sacred) House, (saying), "Associate not anything (in worship) with Me, and sanctify My House for those who compass it round, or stand up, or bow, or prostrate themselves (therein in prayer). And proclaim the Pilgrimage among men: they will come to you on foot and (mounted) on every kind of camel, lean on account of journeys through deep and distant mountain highways."

Pilgrims to Mecca symbolize their purification for the journey in their appearance. Men wear sandals and wrap themselves in two pieces of unsewn white cloth, called the ihram. Some men shave their heads. Women wear a simple version of their normal clothing or a long white dress, with only their hands and faces showing. These plain garments symbolize the

This illustration from an ancient Persian manuscript depicts Muslim pilgrims arriving at the Ka'aba during the Hajj.

Pilgrims to Mecca wear simple white garments. These symbolize the fact that all Muslims are equal in Allah's sight.

equality of all before Allah—Muslims do not observe class or cultural differences among those making the pilgrimage. Both Shiite and Sunni Muslims participate in the Hajj together, and are expected to live in harmony during this time.

First Day of the Hajj

The Hajj begins on the eighth day of Dhu al-Hijja. The pilgrims enter the Grand Mosque of Mecca (al-Masjid al-Haram), and walk seven times around the ancient shrine known as the Ka'aba. The pilgrims walk around the shrine in a counter-clockwise direction; this is known as *tawaf* (circling). As they pass the eastern corner of the Ka'aba, the pilgrims attempt to kiss a black stone that is framed in silver and set into the shrine's wall. Pilgrims that cannot get close enough to kiss the stone will point to it as they walk past.

The black stone (known as al-Hajr al-Aswad) may have been part of an ancient meteorite; according to Islamic tradition, it fell from Heaven to show Adam and Eve where to build an altar to God. The Patriarch Abraham is said to have incorporated the stone into the wall when he rebuilt the Ka'aba with his son Ishmael. Muslims believe that at one time, the stone was pure white; it turned black over time because it absorbs the sins of those who take part in the Hajj.

After completing *tawaf*, pilgrims perform a ritual known as *sa'ee*. This involves walking or running seven times between two low hills near the Ka'aba. This is meant to re-enact the search for water by Ishmael's mother, Hagar. This event is described in the Bible (Genesis 21:14–19). According to Islamic tradition, Hagar searched desperately for water until the Angel Gabriel revealed the sacred well called Zamzam. As part of the ritual, pilgrims drink water from the Zamzam well. Once this is done, the pilgrims return to their tents at the nearby town of Mina.

Second Day of the Hajj

On the ninth day of Dhu al-Hijja, the pilgrims leave their tents at Mina for Mount Arafat. It was here that the Prophet Muhammad is said to have given his last sermon to the Muslim community, in 632 C.E. Muslims spend the afternoon and evening on Mount Arafat in contemplative vigil. Most people use this time to pray, or to reflect on their lives.

After the sun sets, pilgrims leave Arafat for Muzdalifah, an open, level area to the southeast of Mina. There, they gather pebbles or small stones that can be used the next day in another ritual. Because of the crowds at the Hajj, many pilgrims do not

(continued on page 34)

Tent cities like this are constructed at Mina and Medina to accommodate the millions of pilgrims who travel from hundreds of countries to participate in the Hajj each year. Citizens of Mecca refer to the pilgrims as *duyuf al-rahman*, "guests of the Merciful [God]."

(continued from page 31)

arrive at Muzdalifah until late at night. Many camp there, returning to Mina the next morning.

Stoning of the Devil

The tenth day of Dhu al-Hijja begins the ritual called *Ramy al-Jamarat*, or "Stoning of the Devil." According to Islamic tradition, when Allah told Abraham to sacrifice his son, the devil appeared three times and tried to convince the patriarch not to obey. Each time, Abraham refused; in fact, he threw stones at the Devil to drive him away.

Three walls have been constructed in Mina for this ritual; before 2005, Muslims flung stones at three pillars. On the tenth of Dhu al-Hijja, Pilgrims throw seven pebbles at the largest wall. On both the eleventh and twelfth days of the month, they throw seven pebbles at all three of the walls. Thus a total of 49 pebbles are needed to complete this ritual, since this is believed to be the

Pilgrims chant as they walk up Mount Arafat. Muslims believe that Muhammad preached his final sermon from this mountain.

Pilgrims throw pebbles at one of the walls constructed near the Jamaraat Bridge in Mina. The walls were built in 2005 to make the "stoning of the devil" ritual safer; before this, pilgrims some-times missed the pillars and hit people on the other side.

number of days during which Abraham was tempted by the Devil. Pilgrims throw pebbles from a structure called the Jamaraat Bridge.

The stoning ritual is the most dangerous part of the Hajj. People have been crushed by the large crowds around the Jamaraat Bridge. In 2006, more than 360 pilgrims were killed in a stampede at the bridge. A similar incident in 2004 led to more than 250 deaths. In recent years the Saudi government has implemented safety regulations and rebuilt the bridge to make it less dangerous.

'Eid Al-Adha

Whether or not they are participating in the Hajj, Muslims also celebrate a festival known as 'Eid al-Adha (Feast of the Sacrifice) on the tenth of Dhu al-Hijja. The festival commemorates Abraham's willingness to obey Allah by sacrificing his son. According to Muslim traditions, Allah told Abraham to take his son Ishmael into the mountains and prepare him to be sacri-ficed. Abraham did this as Allah commanded. He built an altar, tied his son's hands, and raised his knife to sacrifice Ishmael to Allah. Before Abraham could bring the knife down, Allah ordered him to stop, free his son, and sacrifice a ram instead.

On 'Eid al-Adha, Muslims remember the patriarch Abraham's willingness to completely obey all of Allah's commands—even his order to sacrifice his son. Pleased at Abraham's obedience, Allah sends an angel to prevent the sacrifice, and tells Abraham to sacrifice a ram instead. The story of Abraham is told in both the Bible and the Qur'an, but there is an important difference in the two accounts. Muslims believe that Abraham was told to sacrifice his older son, Ishmael, from whom the Arabs are said to be descended. Jews and Christians believe that Abraham was told to sacrifice his younger son, Isaac, a forefather of the Hebrew people. The event has been depicted in many sculptures and artworks, including this 17th-century painting by the Dutch master Rembrandt.

An important part of the 'Eid al-Adha celebration is the sacrifice of animals—typically sheep, goats, or cows—to commemorate Abraham's sacrifice. In the past, pilgrims performed the sacrifices themselves. Today, many pilgrims purchase vouchers in Mecca before the Hajj begins. This allows an animal to be slaughtered in their name during 'Eid al-Adha. The slaughter takes place in a large facility, with the butchers carefully observing *halal* restrictions. The meat is packaged and distributed to poor people around the world. This fulfills another of the requirements of 'Eid al-Adha: the duty to help Muslims who are less fortunate.

Muslims who are not on the Hajj celebrate 'Eid al-Adha by putting on their best clothing and attending their local mosque for a special prayer and a short sermon. Afterward, people visit at the mosque or socialize in the homes of family and friends, where they eat large meals of dishes prepared especially for the feast. Children are often given gifts and sweets. The traditional greeting is *'Eid Mubarak!*, which means "holiday blessings."

Muslims who can afford to purchase an animal for sacrifice (often a sheep) will have them slaughtered, often in a public place. The meat is traditionally distributed in three parts—one part for the poor, one part as a gift to friends and extended family, and one part for the immediate family. Muslim families that cannot afford the expense of sacrificing a sheep may simply purchase meat to eat and give away.

Malaysian Muslims slaughter a cow for an 'Eid al-Adha feast. The butchers must be careful to properly observe Muslim dietary restrictions so the meat will be considered *halal*.

Completing the Hajj

On the tenth or eleventh of Dhu al-Hijja, Muslim pilgrims go back to the Grand Mosque in Mecca and perform another tawaf, circling the Ka'aba seven times. On the eleventh and twelfth days, the pilgrims are required to perform the stoning ritual in Mina again.

In their spare time, some Muslims travel north to the city of Medina, where Muhammad established the first Muslim community in the seventh century. These pilgrims visit the Prophet's

Pilgrims to Mecca often visit the nearby city of Medina, where Muhammad established the first Muslim community in 622 c.e. The tomb of Muhammad is located in this mosque, as are tombs or shrines to several other important early leaders of Islam.

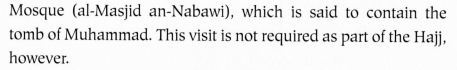

Mosque (al-Masjid an-Nabawi), which is said to contain the tomb of Muhammad. This visit is not required as part of the Hajj, however.

Pilgrims must depart Mina for Mecca before sunset on the twelfth of Dhu al-Hijja. If they are unable to leave Mina before sunset, they must perform the stoning ritual again on the thirteenth before returning to Mecca. Before leaving Mecca, pilgrims perform a farewell *tawaf* called the *Tawaf al-Wada*.

The rituals of the Hajj are meant to symbolize the unity of the global Muslim community. The pilgrimage emphasizes commitment, obedience to Allah's will, and self-sacrifice. Those who have completed the Hajj are often honored in their communities. For nearly every Muslim who makes the trip, the Hajj is a life-changing event. People from all nations and races, rich and poor, become equals when they travel to Mecca. Making the journey reminds them of the importance of faith in their lives and the need to respect their fellow Muslims.

Pilgrims can also visit Mecca and perform the tawaf and other rituals at other times of the year. This is sometimes called the *Umrah*, or "lesser pilgrimage." However, Muslims who perform the *Umrah* are still obligated to perform the Hajj at some time if they are physically and financially able. Once someone fulfills the obligation to perform the Hajj, they are referred to by the honorific title Hajj, followed by their name.

Births, Weddings, and Deaths

amily life is very important to Muslims. All Muslim societies have developed specific rituals and traditions to celebrate and observe important events related to the cycle of life: weddings, births, and deaths.

Births in the Muslim World

A newborn baby quickly receives an initiation into Islam. As soon as the umbilical cord is cut, many Muslims follow a tradition of whispering the Muslim call to prayer—the same words the child will hear from the local mosque five times each day— in each ear. Other parents may whisper other things, such as the first chapter of the Qur'an, into the child's ear.

One simple rite that some Muslims perform to welcome a new baby is to give him or her a taste of something sweet. It is traditional for parents to chew a date and rub the juice along the baby's gums. Muslims believe that the Prophet Muhammad did this with his own children, and that this will help the infant's digestion.

To give thanks for the birth, some parents may follow an old custom of shaving the baby's head and giving the poor an amount of gold or silver equal to the weight of the hair. In some societies, a sheep or other animal is slaughtered and eaten in celebration of the birth as part of a special celebration called *aqiqa*.

Parents typically name their baby between seven and forty days after birth in a special ceremony with relatives and friends. (If the baby is to be circumcised, this is also done on the seventh day after the baby's birth.) *Shari'a* (Islamic law) provides guidelines for parents in choosing names, which all have meanings. A name may describe a positive quality about the child, or express the wishes of the parent for the child. Parents may also name their children after Muhammad or other prophets or heroes of Islamic history. The name cannot be tasteless, offensive, or indicate that the child serves anyone other than Allah. Some common Arabic

Muslim children begin learning about their religion from an early age.

names for boys include Abdallah ("servant of Allah"), Ali ("excellent"), and Karim ("generous"). A common formula for male Muslim names is 'Abd al _____ (usually an attribute of God), meaning "servant of the _____." Some popular girls' names include Fatima (this was the name of a daughter of Muhammad), Nawal ("gift"), and Iman ("faith").

Because religious identity is patrilineal in Islam, sons are often referred to as ibn or bin ("the son of" followed by their father's name), and fathers are abu or abi ("the father of" followed by their son's name). Prominent figures in Islamic history and contemporary politics are known by their *kunya* (nickname), such as the Caliph Abu Bakr, or Abu Mazen (the popular name for the current president of the Palestinian Authority, Mahmoud Abbas).

A child born to Muslim parents will learn about his or her religion on a daily basis. Among the first words taught to many children are, "In the name of Allah, the Merciful, the Compassionate." With these words, Muslims affirm their connection to Allah in their daily lives. This phrase (*bismi-llahi ar-rahman ar-raheem*) is known as the *basmala* in Arabic. Children see their parents praying and join in the prayers after learning how they are performed. Parents are responsible for ensuring that their children understand their religion, in addition to teaching them manners and proper behavior.

A small number of Muslims do not observe annual birthdays of their children, saying that they celebrate people rather than Allah. Most Muslims in the United States and elsewhere celebrate birthdays, however. As a compromise, some Muslim parents take birthdays as an opportunity to teach their children to thank God for giving them life and good health. In the United States, it is customary for Muslim children to have parties and receive presents on their birthdays.

Wedding Traditions

Weddings are joyous celebrations for families in the Islamic world. Nearly all Muslim weddings are large affairs that involve many people and can last for days. In many Muslim communities, the newlyweds hold an elaborate feast that may last up to a week. The extended families of both bride and groom attend, and local poor people are often invited to share in the feast as well. The bride, and sometimes also the groom, will usually dress in rich, colorful clothes.

Young Muslim men and women may choose to marry after meeting socially and falling in love. However, in some rural Muslim societies, traditional arranged marriages, in which parents choose who their children will marry, still occur. Islamic law decrees the young couple must agree to the match.

Even when a young Muslim meets a potential marriage partner, there are strict rules regulating the time they can spend together. Western-style dating is particularly rare in rural areas. Instead, young single men and women often meet in a group setting, then ask their families to help them find out more about a person that interests them. In cosmopolitan urban centers, like Cairo, Damascus, or Beirut, men and women who are engaged will often go out together, although they are expected to stay in public places.

Before a couple is married, the families of the bride and groom generally negotiate a marriage contract that may include a payment of money or valuables to the bride called a *mahr* (dowry). The bride either saves the dowry as financial security for herself, or she may spend the dowry on helping to prepare the marital home. Islamic law, however, strongly recommends that the bride not spend the dowry on preparing the marital home and forbids the family of the bride from taking the dowry

Although Islamic law provides guidelines for courtship and marriage, social customs regarding romantic relationships vary from region to region.

or spending it on themselves. (In practice this restriction is often violated, especially in poor countries.)

Some Muslims marry early in life. In Iran, for example, young men can be married at age fourteen and girls at age nine. A 2001 report by UNICEF stated that in predominantly Muslim countries in Africa, Asia, and the Middle East, many girls are married between the ages of 14 and 18. This is particularly true of Muslims living traditional lifestyles.

The wide variety of Muslim wedding traditions throughout the world reflects the broad cultural differences in the Islamic world. Celebrations often follow local customs that may predate Islam. In countries like Malaysia or Afghanistan, the couple sits on thrones and is treated like royalty on their wedding day. Before many Muslim weddings in South Asian countries like India, Pakistan, or Bangladesh, a temporary dye called henna is painted in elaborate designs on the hands of the bride and groom. Some Muslims in Sudan celebrate a marriage with races, contests, and dancing with swords. In

An Indian woman shows off the ornate henna tattoos painted onto her hands and arms before her wedding. This is a cultural practice common to South Asia, rather than a custom required by Islam.

the United Arab Emirates, the bride stays at home and has no visitors for 40 days before the wedding day, when she is covered from head to toe with perfumes and oils. A bride in Palestine may wear a headdress made from hundreds of coins. A newly married husband in Yemen follows an old wedding tradition when he tries to step on his wife's foot as they enter their house. If he succeeds, it is considered a sign that he will rule the house. If she pulls her foot away in time, she will be the boss.

Deaths and Funerals

When a Muslim is near death, family members and friends are expected to comfort the person, reminding him or her about Allah's mercy and forgiveness. Muslims believe that death is a departure from the life of this world, but not the end of a person's

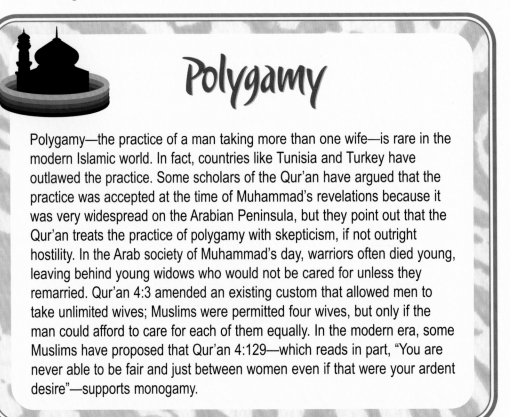

Polygamy

Polygamy—the practice of a man taking more than one wife—is rare in the modern Islamic world. In fact, countries like Tunisia and Turkey have outlawed the practice. Some scholars of the Qur'an have argued that the practice was accepted at the time of Muhammad's revelations because it was very widespread on the Arabian Peninsula, but they point out that the Qur'an treats the practice of polygamy with skepticism, if not outright hostility. In the Arab society of Muhammad's day, warriors often died young, leaving behind young widows who would not be cared for unless they remarried. Qur'an 4:3 amended an existing custom that allowed men to take unlimited wives; Muslims were permitted four wives, but only if the man could afford to care for each of them equally. In the modern era, some Muslims have proposed that Qur'an 4:129—which reads in part, "You are never able to be fair and just between women even if that were your ardent desire"—supports monogamy.

A Muslim cemetery in Fez, Morocco. Funerals in Muslim lands are performed according to Islamic regulations.

existence. Those who have faithfully submitted to Allah's will are admitted to heaven, and at the end of time Allah will judge the lives of all people. This is said to take place on *Yawm ad-Din* (the Day of Judgment) or *Yawm al-Qiyamah* (the Day of Resurrection), which is God's final assessment of humanity.

Upon hearing of a person's death, Muslims often utter the phrase, "From God we have come, and to God we will return." Muslims take special steps to preparing the bodies of the deceased for their return to the creator. In Muslim lands, specific people in each community are trained to prepare bodies for burial. In this special ritual, bodies are washed in a sequence much like the ablution for prayer. They are neither embalmed nor dressed up. Rather, they are wrapped very simply in white, organic cloth called kafan, which is often scented with a sweet perfume. Sometimes, the prepared body is taken to the mosque, where Muslims gather for a special funeral prayer called *jinaza* (or *janaza*). This prayer can also be performed at the burial site.

According to Islamic tradition, Muslims should be buried within a day of their death. Bodies are buried facing Mecca. If possible, a Muslim is buried directly in the earth without a coffin; however, this is not permitted in the United States and some other countries. Typically, a Muslim's grave will only have a small marker.

The relatives and friends of a deceased Muslim are expected to observe a three-day mourning period. During this time mourners are expected to pray for the deceased and visit with those who wish to offer condolences. Mourners must dress simply and avoid jewelry or ornamentation. Qur'an 2:234 specifies that widows must observe a longer mourning period of four months and ten days; during this time the widow may not wear decorative clothing, move from her home, or remarry.

Other Celebrations

In addition to the major festivals of Islam—'Eid al-Adha and 'Eid al-Fitr—many Muslims commemorate important events in the history of Islam. These include Mawlid an-Nabi, Laylat al-Isra' and al-Miraj, Laylat at-Tawbah, Ashura, and al-Hijra. Though these celebrations are very popular in many parts of the world, they are not proscribed in the Qur'an or Hadith. As a result, some Muslims consider them recent innovations that should not count as religious holidays.

Muhammad's Birthday

Though no verifiable record exists of the exact date of Muhammad's birth, Muslims around the world celebrate the Prophet's birthday on the twelfth day of Rabi'a al-Awwal, the third month of the Islamic calendar. This celebration is commonly known as Mawlid an-Nabi ("birth of the Prophet").

This celebration probably began in Egypt during the tenth century, when believers began performing special chants and festivities to mark Muhammad's birth, and it has become one of the most popular innovative celebrations in Islam. It is a major holiday in some countries, including Egypt, Turkey, and Pakistan. However, more conservative states like Saudi Arabia do not observe Mawlid an-Nabi, because the early Muslim community did not celebrate it.

No special prayers or religious services are conducted on this day, but Muslims express their love for Muhammad by gathering to listen to speeches and poems celebrating the Prophet's life and example. In other places, Muslims may also set off fireworks to announce the day, wear new clothes, march in parades, gather with friends and family, and exchange gifts.

Shiite Muslims, who make up about 14 percent of the global Muslim population, observe Muhammad's birthday on the seventeenth day of Rabi'a al-Awwal.

The Night Journey

Many Muslims also celebrate Laylat al-Isra' and al-Miraj, the night of Muhammad's miraculous Night Journey from Mecca to Jerusalem and his ascension into heaven. According to Islamic tradition, the Angel Gabriel visited Muhammad while he slept one night. They filled his heart with wisdom and faith. Then, during the night, Muhammad traveled from Mecca to Jerusalem on a winged horse called al-Buraq (lightning). From the Temple Mount in Jerusalem—the current site of the al-Aqsa mosque—he ascended into heaven, where he visited with earlier prophets of Allah, such as Abraham, Moses, and Jesus. During his time in heaven, Muhammad was told that it would be the duty of Muslims to pray five times a day.

The story is mentioned briefly in Qur'an 17:1 and expounded on at some length in the Hadith. Though the Qur'an mentions no

The silver dome of the al-Aqsa Mosque can be seen atop the structure known as the Temple Mount in Jerusalem. The mosque is built over a rock on which, Muslims believe, Muhammad stood on before ascending to Heaven. Muhammad's "Night Journey" is commemorated each year with the Laylat al-Miraj festival. Muslim children are told the story and pray at the mosque with their parents, then enjoy food and treats.

specific day for this event and no record exists that Muhammad and the early community celebrated this night, Muslims have set the date as the 27th of Rajab, the seventh month of the Islamic calendar. Many mark it with special gatherings in homes and mosques, where the story of Muhammad's Night Journey is told through poetry, chants, and sermons.

The Night of Repentance

The fifteenth of Sha'ban, the month before Ramadan, is considered a "night of repentance." Both Sunni and Shiite Muslims believe this night has special significance. Muslims who celebrate it believe that all who ask Allah for forgiveness on this night will receive it. On this night Muslims are also expected to forgive those who have wronged them. It is also considered a night of preparation for Ramadan.

Ashura

The celebration of Ashura is especially important to Shiites. On this day, they mark the martyrdom of Muhammad's grandson (and Ali's son) Hussein in Karbala by publicly reenacting the events surrounding his death and participating in elaborate mourning rituals, including chest-beating, self-flagellation, and public weeping. Another common tradition in Iran, Iraq, and the Persian Gulf is the staging of passion plays that reenact the Battle of Karbala (680 C.E.), in which Imam Hussein died at the hands of Yazid.

Young Shiite men chant while participating in an Ashura ritual. Shiites consider Ashura a day of mourning, rather than a festival. In countries with large Shiite populations, such as Iran, Iraq, Lebanon, and Bahrain, Ashura is a national holiday.

Shia Muslims walk with their families as part of the Arba'een pilgrimage, February 2009. During Arba'een, which takes place 40 days after Ashura, Shiites travel to Karbala, the site of a battle where Imam Hussein bin Ali was killed in 680 C.E. During the decades that Saddam Hussein ruled Iraq, the Arba'een pilgrimage was forbidden. However, after Saddam's government was overthrown in 2003 by a U.S.-led international coalition, Shiites were once again permitted to make the annual pilgrimage. The number of pilgrims has increased each year; in 2009, it was estimated that more than 12 million Shiites participated in the Arba'een pilgrimage.

The Shiites broke away from the mainstream Sunnis because of a difference over leadership of the Muslim community. When Muhammad died in 632 C.E., he did not leave a male heir, so the Muslims had to choose his successor. The majority of Muslims supported Abu Bakr, a respected friend of Muhammad. However, some backed Ali, the prophet's cousin and son-in-law. These supporters came to be commonly known as Shiites (from *shi'at Ali*, Arabic for "faction/followers of Ali").

Ali eventually caliph, or leader of the Muslim community, in 656. However, the community was torn by civil war, and Ali was

Buildings in Doha, Qatar, are illuminated with colorful lights for a Muslim 'eid, or festival.

assassinated in 661. Ali's death ended what has come to be known as the era of *al-khulafa' ar-rashidun* (the rightly guided caliphs.) These four caliphs, who ruled from 632 to 661 C.E., were Abu Bakr, Umar ibn al-Khattab, Uthman ibn Affan, and Ali ibn Abi Talib. After Ali's death, the Islamic governor of Syria, Muawiya, declared himself caliph and instituted a hereditary dynasty that lasted for nearly a century.

In 680, supporters of Muawiya's son Yazid attacked Ali's son Hussein and his followers at the Battle of Karbala. Hussein and most of his family were killed when he refused to surrender his claim to the caliphate. Imam Hussein's infant son Ali survived, however, so the Shiite line of leadership continued.

Ashura is observed on the tenth day of Muharram, the first month of the Islamic calendar. In countries like Iran, Iraq,

Lebanon, and Bahrain, where Shiites make up a majority of the population, Ashura is a national holiday.

Sunni Muslims also observe Ashura, although not as fervently as Shiites. According to Sunni tradition, the tenth of Muharram is important for reasons other than the martyrdom of Hussein. The day is believed to be the anniversary of a number of other significant occasions in Islamic history, including the day Noah left the ark after the Great Flood and the day on which Muslims were told to pray in the direction of Mecca, rather than Jerusalem.

Muslim New Year

Al-Hijra, the first day of the Islamic year, is celebrated on the first day of Muharram. Though this day is not celebrated in any elaborate way, it remains important to Muslims because it marks the anniversary of Muhammad's journey from Mecca to Medina (the hijra) and was chosen by the second caliph, Umar, to mark the beginning of the Islamic calendar. Muslims are encouraged to think about their beliefs; many will resolve to improve themselves or their relationship with Allah during the new year.

Calendar of Islamic Festivals

1 Muharram ....al-Hijra (Islamic New Year)

10 Muharram ....Ashura

12 Rabi'a al-Awwal ....Mawlid an-Nabi (birthday of the
prophet), Sunni observance

17 Rabi'a al-Awwal ....Mawlid an-Nabi, Shiite observance

27 Rajab ....Laylat al-Isra' and al-Miraj
(Muhammad's Night Journey)

15 Sha'ban ....Muslim night of repentance

1 Ramadan ....period of fasting, required of all
Muslims, begins

27 Ramadan ....Laylat al-Qadr (Night of Power)

1 Shawwal...................Eid al-Fitr (feast of fast-breaking)

8 Duh al-Hijja ....the ritual Hajj pilgrimage begins

10 Duh al-Hijja ....Eid al-Adha (feast of the sacrifice)

Opposite: From a tall minaret, Shiite Muslims can be observed gathering for
Friday prayers at a mosque in Isfahan, Iran.

Glossary

ablution—a cleansing of the body or parts of the body, particularly as a religious ritual.

Allah—the Arabic word for "God."

Arkan al-Islam—The Five Pillars of Islam, which are the shahada (profession of faith), salat (prayer), zakat (charity), sawm (fasting during the holy month of Ramadan), and Hajj (making the pilgrimage to Mecca)

alms—money, food, or other goods given as charity to the poor.

caliph—head of the Caliphate and commander of the community of Muslims

Caliphate—political leadership of the community of Muslims

dowry—money, property, or a pledge of money or property given by a husband to his wife at the time of marriage.

'Eid—holiday or festival, in a general sense.

'Eid al-Adha—a holiday feast during which Muslims remember Abraham's willingness to obey Allah's command to sacrifice his son. When Abraham proved willing, Allah allowed him to sacrifice a ram instead.

'Eid al-Fitr—a holiday feast that marks the end of Ramadan.

Hadith—a collection of statements and actions by Muhammad and his close companions that Muslims use as an example for their own lives.

Hajj—a ritual pilgrimage to Mecca that every Muslim is expected to make. It is also the honofiric title bestowed on someone who performs the ritual pilgrimage

imam—a religious leader associated with a mosque (for Shiites, the historical leaders of Islam who followed in the footsteps of Muhammad).

Islam—the Arabic word meaning "submission" to God, this is the religion founded by Muhammad in the 7th century CE.

khutba—a sermon delivered at a mosque during the communal jumu'a prayer

mosque—a Muslim house of worship, also known in Arabic as a masjid, or a jam'i.

muezzin—the mosque leader who issues the call to prayer at various times each day

Muslim—a person whose religion is Islam

Qur'an—literally "recitation" in Arabic, this is the holy book of Islam viewed by Muslims as the direct word of God as revealed to his Prophet Muhammad. The Qur'an is a key source of Islamic law and practice.

pilgrimage—a journey (often long and difficult) to a shrine or other place of religious significance

polygamy—marriage in which a spouse of either sex may have more than one mate at the same time

qibla—the direction facing Mecca

Ramadan—the holy ninth month in the Islamic calendar when Muslims refrain from eating or drinking during daylight hours. This is meant to be a period of meditation and self-sacrifice.

self-flagellation—punishing oneself physically, especially by whipping.

shari'a—Islamic law.

Shia—the smaller of Islam's two major branches, whose rift with the larger Sunni branch originated with seventh-century disputes over who should succeed Muhammad as leader of the Muslim community.

Shiite—a follower of Shia Islam. Shiites make up about 14 percent of all Muslims.

Sunna—a collection of accepted practice in Islam, based on the life of Muhammad.

Sunni—a Muslim who belongs to the largest branch of Islam, which holds that Muslims should follow the Sunna, or ways, of Muhammad, a tradition that began when the earliest Muslims chose Muhammad's successor.

ummah—the worldwide community of Muslims.

Further Reading

Gulevich, Tanya. *Understanding Islam and Muslim Traditions: An introduction to the Religious Practices, Celebration, Festivals, Observances, Beliefs, Folklore, Customs, and Calendar Systems of the World's Muslim Community*. Detroit: Omnigraphics, 2005.

Jordan, Michael. *Islam: An Illustrated History*. London: Carlton Books, 2002.

Miller, John, and Aaron Kenedi, editors. *Inside Islam: The Faith, the People, and the Conflicts of the World's Fastest Growing Religion*. New York: Marlowe and Co., 2002.

Nimer, Mohamed. *The North American Muslim Resource Guide: Muslim Community Life in the United States and Canada*. New York: Routledge, 2002.

Senker, Cath. *My Muslim Year: A Year of Religious Festivals*. London: Wayland, 2007.

Internet Resources

https://www.cia.gov/library/publications/the-world-factbook

The CIA World Factbook is a convenient source of basic information about any country in the world. This site includes links to a page on each country with geographic, demographic, economic, and governmental data.

http://www.holidays.net/ramadan

All about the celebration of the Muslim month of fasting and reflection and other information about Islam.

http://www.fordham.edu/halsall/islam/islamsbook.html

Links to texts from every period in the history of Islam; also includes a timeline covering the years 500–1999.

http://www.Quran.org

Links to Qur'an resources, including online translations, browsers, and commentary.

http://www.pbs.org/wgbh/pages/frontline/shows/muslims

A special installment of the PBS program Frontline that examines contemporary Islam through profiles of and interviews with Muslims in the United States, Africa, the Middle East, and Asia.

http://www.fpri.org

The Web site of the Foreign Policy Research Institute.

Numbers in **bold italics** refer to captions.